The

Senior's Guide
to End-of-Life Issues
Advance Directives, Wills,
Funerals & Cremations

Check out these other great titles in the Senior's Guide Series!

The Senior's Guide to Digital Photography

The Senior's Guide to Dating (Again)

The Senior's Guide to the Internet

The Senior's Guide to eBay®

The Senior's Guide to Easy Computing

The Senior's Guide to Computer Tips & Tricks

The

Senior's Guide
to End-of-Life Issues

Advance Directives, Wills,
Funerals & Cremations

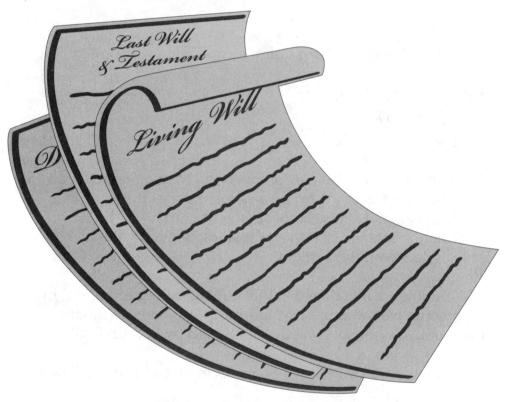

By Rebecca Sharp Colmer,
Certified Senior Advisor (CSA)
and
Todd M. Thomas

EKLEKTIKA PRESS
Chelsea, Michigan

Table of Contents

Table of Contents

Table of Contents

Table of Contents

Table of Contents

Table of Contents

Table of Contents

DISCLAIMER

Every effort has been made to make this book as complete as possible and as accurate as possible. However, there may be mistakes both typographical and in content. Therefore, this text should be used as a general guide and not the ultimate source of information.

PART I

End-of-Life Planning: The Basics

This book contains general information concerning end-of-life issues for seniors, but may not apply to all life situations. It is not meant as a substitute for a thorough understanding of state or federal law or the decisions of courts or public officials or agencies.

This book is an informational guide intended to aid the reader as to the type of issues that should be raised with family, an attorney or appropriate representative. It will provide you with information that you may consider using to establish your preferences regarding end-of-life decisions.

No matter where you are in the process of successful aging, it is important to prepare for what "might" come your way. It is only natural to delay or postpone making plans regarding your death, but doing so only hurts your loved-ones or heirs.

Be proactive and give your family and friends a great gift by planning NOW for your end-of-life issues. Oddly enough, it will give you a good feeling, too.

WHEN SHOULD I START PLANNING FOR END-OF-LIFE DECISIONS?

If you are over age 18 and competent, it is never too early to start planning! At a minimum, everybody should have a Will, a Living Will, and a Durable Power of Attorney for Health Care (DPAHC).

The Durable Power of Attorney for Health Care (a type of advance directive) is probably the most important document that you need to have.

The Durable Power of Attorney for Health Care is for you. The other documents that we will be talking about are more beneficial for your heirs.

Each of these should be reviewed and updated (if necessary) annually. Even though a great deal of self-help is available in print and online, it's a good idea to consult with a lawyer and/or doctor to make sure you have covered all of the bases, legally.

WHAT IS THE BEST WAY TO COMMUNICATE MY DESIRES AND PREFERENCES?

There may come a time when you become too sick to make your own decisions about your personal affairs, including medical, financial, or legal matters. If that happens, then decisions will have to be made for you. If you have not given any instructions, no one will know what you would have decided.

It is important to talk about your wishes AND put them in writing. Don't kid yourself by making excuses, such as:

- I'm not old enough to worry about it.
- It's too depressing to think about.
- I'm too busy to think about such things.
- I've expressed my wishes and it's not necessary to write them down.

Often it is just as difficult for family members to raise these issues as it is for you to voice your wishes.

WHAT DO I HAVE TO LOOK FORWARD TO AS I AGE?

The U.S. Bureau of the Census predicts that by 2030, one in five Americans will be seniors — 70 million people who are 65 and older. That means that your chances of living to age 100 are improving steadily!

Gerontologists predict that the baby boomers will tackle the challenges of aging, head on. There will be a shift of focus from the obsession with youth to an aging-friendly environment.

Now is the time to prepare for the upcoming years, no matter what your age.

WHAT ARE SOME OF THE "AGING RELATED" CHALLENGES SENIORS FACE TODAY?

There are plenty of challenges ranging from small to large. Some of them are:

- Unsafe conditions in the home.
- Understanding new communication technologies such as the Internet. (Read *The Senior's Guide to the Internet*.)
- Hard-to-read signs for streets and businesses.
- A changing family structure or decline of the nuclear family. Many of today's seniors never married nor had children. Many of those who did, are now divorced, separated, widowed or without adult children.
- There are more remarriages and blended families that can affect financial support, care-giving, and housing decisions.
- Loss of relationships and financial independence.
- Chronic illnesses like heart disease, cancer, stroke, arthritis, diabetes.
- Loss of mobility.

WHAT FACTORS MAY INFLUENCE MY DECISIONS ABOUT END-OF-LIFE ISSUES?

How we live our life and how we plan for our death are personal choices. However, society also influences us as we observe the attitudes, ceremonies and rituals that surround death and dying in our culture. For guidance in these important decisions, many people seek religious or spiritual advice.

Medical technology and medical practice have changed how patients, lawmakers, physicians, ethicists and society in general think about and define life, death and dying.

WHAT END-OF-LIFE ISSUES SHOULD I START PLANNING FOR TODAY?

Whatever else you do, you should have the following:

1. Advance Directives which include a Durable Power of Attorney for Health Care and a Living Will.
2. An updated and valid Will.
3. A Durable Power of Attorney.

WHAT OTHER ADVANCE PLANNING SHOULD I CONSIDER BEYOND LEGAL AND MEDICAL DOCUMENTS?

Frequent discussions among family members regarding your last wishes, are extremely important. It is also important to tell someone where your important papers are kept.

It is very helpful to grieving family members to have a file that includes:

- List of all family members, including full names and addresses.
- List of prior marriages.
- List of bank accounts, complete with numbers.
- List of insurance policies, complete with numbers.
- List of assets and business interests.
- List of all assets in investment accounts.
- List of credit cards, with numbers.
- Location of safe deposit boxes and keys.
- List of information pertinent to weekly, monthly, or fiscal actions.
- List of points of contact, with a phone number, for each outside agency your successors may have to interact with (such as the Social Security Administration or a bank).

WHAT IS A GUARDIANSHIP?

Guardianship is a legal method used to insure that a person who is unable to make decisions on their own has someone specifically assigned to make decisions on their behalf. A person for whom a guardian is appointed is known as a ward.

A guardian can be given the power to choose where a ward will live; to consent to medical treatment; to receive money and property belonging to the ward; and to apply this money toward the ward's support and care.

The guardian must make regular reports to the court. Guardian status ends automatically with the ward's death, but can also be ended by the court if the ward's assets run out or if the guardian becomes unable or unwilling to fulfill his or her duties.

An alternative to guardian/ward relationship is for one individual to have a power of attorney for another. Power of attorney can be extensive or limited and can range from the most basic control over decisions such as selling a house, to wider-ranging control over general financial and legal decisions. (See page 23).

WHAT IS A CONSERVATOR?

A conservator is a person or corporation appointed by probate court to manage another person's property and financial affairs. This differs from a guardian, who is appointed by probate court and makes the decisions about the care of another person.

Unlike a guardianship, a conservator cannot make health care decisions.

WHAT IS THE DIFFERENCE BETWEEN POWER OF ATTORNEY AND DURABLE POWER OF ATTORNEY?

A power of attorney is a document which gives another person the power to handle some or all of your financial affairs. An ordinary power of attorney ends when you become mentally incapable because of sickness or injury to handle your affairs. A durable power of attorney does not end in these circumstances.

A Durable Power of Attorney allows you to delegate broad authority over your personal financial affairs, even and especially when you become disabled or incompetent. This kind of power of attorney takes effect immediately; it does not wait until disability. So it's possible, in theory, for the attorney-in-fact to act independently, behind your back, even if you're healthy. Presumably, of course, your attorney-in-fact is trustworthy beyond reproach. If there is any doubt about this, perhaps the Durable Power of Attorney is just not for you.

A Durable Power of Attorney can begin when you sign it or it can be triggered into effect at a later date, or under certain circumstances as stated by you.

All powers of attorney, ordinary or durable, generally cease when the person granting the power dies.

IS THERE ANY WAY TO PLAN FOR GRIEF AND LOSS?

Yes and no. Knowledge and understanding of the grief process may help you come to terms with death, in general.

In our culture, we have a ritual for death — the funeral. Funerals tend to help survivors heal emotionally. It gives survivors a chance to gather and recall and recognize the importance the deceased had in their lives.

However, everyone grieves in their own way, and in their own time. In this respect, no two people grieve exactly the same way.

PART 2

End-of-Life Health Care Concerns

It is important to learn about the options for your end-of-life care, and equally important to comprehend the recommendations that your health care team provides.

There are many resources and support services available to you, your family, and caregivers for assistance with decision-making and overall coping.

Most seniors facing the end-of-life stage want pain and symptom control, to avoid inappropriate prolongation of the dying process, to relieve burdens on family and caregivers, to strengthen relationships with loved ones, and to achieve a sense of control.

I'M HEALTHY, WHY SHOULD I WORRY ABOUT END-OF-LIFE PLANNING?

When you're healthy, it's hard to think about the care you want at the end of your life. However, it may be the best time to make these decisions.

An accident or serious illness can happen any time. Talking with your doctor now gives you a chance to ask questions and talk about your concerns. If you do this when you're healthy, you'll be thinking clearly as you talk about this important topic.

WHAT ARE THE AMERICAN LONGEVITY STATISTICS?

Life expectancy in the United States is at an all-time high, according to recent reports from the Centers for Disease Control and Prevention.

Deaths from heart disease, cancer and diabetes are down, contributing to an average life expectancy of 77.6 years for Americans. In 1900, the average lifespan was 47.3 years. Among those 85 and older, there are five women for every two men. [See *The Senior's Guide to Dating (Again)*].

Americans turning 65 today will live, on average, an additional 18 years.

The oldest old (85+) is the fastest growing segment of the American Senior population, at 4.2 million. As a result, the need for health care and related services is exploding.

One-fourth of senior citizens age 65-74 and one-half of those 75+ reported a limitation caused by a chronic illness such as diabetes or arthritis.

WHAT IS PALLIATIVE CARE?

Palliative Care is care given to people with chronic, often life-threatening illnesses, or after it becomes obvious that no cure is possible.

Palliative Care focuses on symptom management, enhancing quality of life and/or psychosocial needs.

Palliative Care affirms life and views dying as a normal process. It neither hastens nor postpones death, yet it provides relief from pain and other distressing symptoms.

Palliative Care includes treatment that enhances comfort and improves the quality of an individual's life during the last phase of life. No specific therapy is excluded from consideration.

Pain management is a key component of good palliative care, rather than affecting the underlying disease.

MAY I CHOOSE PALLIATIVE CARE OVER CONVENTIONAL MEDICAL CARE?

Yes, you have that choice. Aggressive pain management is an essential component of palliative care intended to provide relief from physical suffering at the end-of-life.

All health care interventions, whether palliative or conventional therapy, are delivered at a price. Assessing the cost of interventions does not mean that less intervention, or more intervention, is better. In other words, more money doesn't mean better care and less suffering.

MAY I HAVE MEDICAL TREATMENT WITHDRAWN OR WITHHELD?

Withholding or withdrawing life-sustaining treatment is an ethically and legally accepted practice, in most states, and may be specified in Advance Directives.

It allows patients to forego or terminate life-sustaining equipment in order to let nature run its course.

There are many reasons to choose this option. Some include: maintaining control over the dying process, reducing medical expenses that are futile, relieving the burden on loved ones.

WHAT IS THE DIFFERENCE BETWEEN ASSISTED SUICIDE, PHYSICIAN-ASSISTED SUICIDE, AND EUTHANASIA?

"Assisted suicide" refers to the situation in which persons request the help of others, in the form of access to information or means (actual help), in order to end their own lives.

"Physician-assisted suicide" (PAS) is the voluntary termination of one's own life by administration of a lethal substance with the direct or indirect assistance of a physician.

"Euthanasia" generally is when someone intentionally takes a person's life with a stated intent to alleviate or prevent perceived suffering.

Physician-assisted suicide is illegal in every state except Oregon. Assisted suicide and euthanasia are illegal in the United States.

WHAT IS THE DIFFERENCE BETWEEN DOUBLE EFFECT AND TERMINAL SEDATION?

The "double effect" is a term given to the practice of providing large doses of medication to relieve pain even if the unintended side effect of such medication may be to hasten death.

"Terminal sedation" is the term given to the practice of administering sufficient pain medication to render a dying person who is experiencing severe, intractable pain, unconscious through an artificial coma. In many cases, artificial nutrition and hydration are also withheld or withdrawn, and unconsciousness is maintained until death occurs.

WHAT IS A HASTENED DEATH?

"Hastened death" is one of those terms that generate confusion and controversy because of lack of consensus about descriptive terminology.

Broadly, it means to end one's life earlier than would have happened without intervention. Some use it to refer to assisted suicide and euthanasia only, while others include it in the category of withholding and withdrawing treatment — death caused by aggressive pain management, and voluntary cessation of eating and drinking.

WHAT IS HOSPICE CARE?

The focus of hospice is care, not cure. Think of it as a subset of palliative care. It is a program of supportive care services providing physical, psychological, social, and spiritual care for dying persons, their families, and other loved ones.

Most hospice services are available in both the home and in-patient settings. Home hospice care is provided either on a part time, intermittent, regularly scheduled, or around the clock basis.

In the United States, hospice patients have received a terminal diagnosis and generally have less than six months to live.

According to the Hospice Foundation of America, there are over 3000 hospices in the United States. Approximately two-thirds of hospice patients are over the age of 65.

Hospice care is a covered benefit under Medicare and is funded by Medicaid in at least 36 states.

HOW IS HOSPICE CARE DIRECTED?

Usually, a family member serves as the primary caregiver and, when appropriate, helps make decisions for the terminally-ill individual. Members of the hospice staff make regular visits to assess the patient and provide additional care or other services. Hospice staff members are on-call 24 hours a day, seven days a week.

The hospice team develops a care plan that meets each patient's individual needs for pain management and symptom control. The team usually consists of:

- The patient's personal physician.
- Hospice physician (or medical director).
- Nurses.
- Home health aides.
- Social workers.
- Clergy or other counselors.
- Trained volunteers.
- Speech, physical, and occupational therapists, if needed.

WHAT SERVICES DO THE HOSPICE
TEAM PROVIDE?

Among its major responsibilities, the interdisciplinary hospice team:

- Manages the patient's pain and symptoms.
- Assists the patient with the emotional, psychosocial and spiritual aspects of dying.
- Provides needed drugs, medical supplies, and equipment.
- Coaches the family on how to care for the patient.
- Delivers special services such as speech and physical therapy when needed.
- Makes short-term inpatient care available when pain or symptoms become too difficult to manage at home, or the caregiver needs respite time.
- Provides bereavement care and counseling to surviving family and friends.

WHO IS ELIGIBLE FOR HOSPICE CARE?

Hospice care is for any person who has a life-threatening or terminal illness. Most reimbursement sources require a prognosis of six months or less to live if the illness runs its normal course.

Some think hospice is only for cancer patients. Not so. Patients with both cancer and non-cancer illnesses are eligible to receive hospice care. All hospices consider the patient and family together as the unit of care.

WHAT DOES "DEATH WITH DIGNITY" MEAN?

Let's face it; we're all going to die someday. Most people hope for a "simple, pain-free, good death," however they may define it.

The process of dying is often influenced by individual cultures. "Death with dignity" is a cultural response to the technology that prolongs life. Technology often takes away our ability to choose and participate in the way we will experience the end of our life.

The decision to end one's life when death is approaching anyway is sometimes called self-deliverance, rational suicide, physician-assisted suicide (PAS), or voluntary euthanasia; this is a special case of the more general topic of suicide. The "right to die" is the subject of controversial legal battles on an international scale.

PART 3

Advance Directives and Living Wills

This section of the book answers questions about the importance of Advance Directives. The Advance Directive, including Durable Power of Attorney for Health Care (DPAHC) and Living Will directly affects the quality of your life and the quality of your death.

The term "Advance Directive" is the generic name for a document that expresses an individual's preferences regarding the acceptance or rejection of medical treatment under certain medical conditions in the event that he/she subsequently becomes unable to make decisions or express his/her wishes.

Many people often have misinformation or a misunderstanding about directives. All end-of-life choices and medical decisions have complex components and consequences that could directly impact your end of life.

WHAT IS AN ADVANCE DIRECTIVE?

An "Advance Directive" is a legal document that tells doctors and health care providers how you want them to carry out medical decisions you have made for future crisis care, if you cannot communicate these decisions for yourself. An Advance Directive is:

- An instruction such as a Durable Power of Attorney for Health Care (DPAHC).
- A directive in accordance with patient self-determination initiatives.
- A Living Will.
- An oral directive which states either a person's choices for medical treatment or, in the event the person is unable to make treatment choices, designates who will make those decisions.

Under the law in most states, Advance Directives are documents signed by a competent person, over age 18, giving direction to health care pro-viders about treatment choices in certain circum-stances. If a person becomes incapacitated and is no longer capable of making his or her own deci-sions then an Advance Directive may be used.

A good Advance Directive describes the kind of treatment you would want depending on how sick you are and unlikely to recover, or if you are permanently unconscious. Advance Directives usually tell your doctor that you don't want certain kinds of treatment. However, they can also say that you want a certain treatment no matter how ill you are.

There are two basic types of Advance Directives: a Durable Power Of Attorney for Health Care (DPAHC) and a Living Will.

WHY SHOULD I HAVE AN ADVANCE DIRECTIVE?

You probably have strong feelings about the kind of medical treatment or care you would like to receive or refuse in certain circumstances. An Advance Directive lets you succinctly state your feelings.

Most people put off writing an Advance Directive. All too often it is not the patient, but a family member, who ends up making treatment decisions simply because you did not take the time to write an Advance Directive.

You are not required by law to have an Advance Directive. A recent Gallup Poll found that nearly 60 percent of Americans haven't prepared any form of Advance Directive.

WHAT ARE MY RIGHTS AS A PATIENT?

As an adult in a hospital, skilled nursing facility, or other health care setting, you have a right to:

- Keep your personal and medical records private.
- Know what kind of medical treatment you will receive.
- Tell people ahead of time what type of treatment you want, or don't want, in case you lose the ability to speak for yourself.

You can make treatment choices as long as you are a competent adult and can communicate.

WHAT HAPPENS IF I BECOME UNABLE TO MAKE OR EXPRESS MY HEALTH CARE DECISIONS?

If you are no longer competent, but you have made sure your family and caregivers know what you would want, it will be easier to follow your wishes. If you have not made your wishes known to family and care-givers, a court may have to name a guardian (refer to page 21) to make decisions for you.

As was shown in a recent legal/medical case in Florida, different family members may have different ideas about what you want. **That is why written directives are superior to verbal instructions.**

Having an Advance Directive does not affect the quality of your care or affect life or health insurance. It states what your wishes are in case you cannot speak for yourself.

WHAT IS THE PATIENT SELF-DETERMINATION ACT?

Congress passed this act in 1990. The PSDA formalized a form of communication known as "advance directives for health care."

These written directives are the means by which you inform health care providers of your beliefs and desires regarding health care procedures and treatments, if you are unable to communicate with them.

HOW SHOULD ADVANCE DIRECTIVES BE DOCUMENTED?

In most states, Advance Directives [both Durable Powers of Attorney for Health Care (DPAHC) and Living Wills)] need to be notarized. You will need to sign them in front of witnesses, and have the witnesses sign the document in front of a notary in order for it to be legal and binding. Banks and other businesses have notaries who can do this.

Because of the gravity and importance of these documents, witnesses are required to verify that an Advance Directive document states the true intentions of the maker. Also, witnesses must not have any stake in your estate. They must be people you do not intend to give something to after your death.

Under the law of many states, anyone who could potentially gain by your death is disallowed as a witness. These may include:

- Your physician.
- A health care provider or their employees.
- A health facility operator or their employees.
- Anyone related to you by blood, marriage or adoption.
- Anyone entitled to any part of your estate under an existing will or by operation of law.

IS THERE A STANDARD FORM FOR AN ADVANCE DIRECTIVE?

No. You may use a form designed by an organization, you may hire a lawyer to draft one for you, or you may write your own. You must sign the document, date it and have it witnessed and notarized.

Advance Directives can be very specific or very broad. The best approach is to give enough control to the person you trust, so that they can act sufficiently as your advocate. Be specific about the topics that are of concern to you so that there is no debate about personal discretion.

If you have selected someone to act as your patient advocate, the person accepting the responsibility to act as a patient advocate must sign the designating document.

IF I WRITE AN ADVANCE DIRECTIVE, CAN I CHANGE MY MIND LATER?

Yes! An Advance Directive can be changed or revoked. You must inform your treating health care provider personally or in writing. Completing a new Advance Directive will revoke all previous directives. In addition, if you revoke or change your directive, you should notify every person or facility that has a copy of your prior directive and provide them with a new one.

You should complete a new form if you want to name a different person as your agent or make other changes. However, if you need only to update the address or telephone numbers of your agent or alternate agent(s), you may write in the new information and initial and date the change. Of course, you should make copies or otherwise ensure that those who need this new contact information will have it.

Ideally, an Advance Directive should be reviewed yearly and updated as necessary.

IS AN ADVANCE DIRECTIVE THE SAME THING AS A HEALTH CARE DIRECTIVE?

Yes. In fact, sometimes you will even see it referred to as an Advance Health Care Directive or a Health Care Proxy.

Remember, the term "Advance Directive" is the generic name for a document that reduces to written form an individual's preferences regarding the acceptance or rejection of medical treatment *under certain medical conditions* in the event that he/she subsequently becomes unable to make decisions or express his/her wishes. An Advance Directive permits the individual to decide in advance whether or not to die a natural death, without the application of heroic measures or advanced medical technology, given a particular set of circumstances.

The terminology used to describe the instrument involving end-of-life decisions also varies from state to state. Terms used in statutes and professional literature include "living will," "advance directive," "medical directive," "terminal care document," and "directive to physicians."

WILL OTHER STATES HONOR MY
ADVANCE DIRECTIVE?

Laws governing Advance Directives differ from state to state. If you live in one state, but travel to other states frequently, you may want to consider having your Advance Directive meet the laws of other states. Check with an attorney.

If you travel, you should probably carry a copy of your Advance Directive, just for your own peace of mind.

COULD A FRIEND JUST DECIDE FOR ME WITHOUT AN ADVANCE DIRECTIVE?

No. Laws are really strict about this. Hospitals and other health care providers usually will not let a friend decide unless he or she is named in an Advance Directive. Without an Advance Directive, your friend may have to go to court to have a treatment stopped.

WHAT ISSUES OR DECISIONS SHOULD I CONSIDER BEFORE WRITING AN ADVANCE DIRECTIVE?

The more issues you consider the better. Speak to your doctor before making an Advance Directive so that he or she can explain treatment options. Here are a few issues to get you thinking:

- Are you afraid of dying?
- Who would you like to make treatment decisions for you, if you are unable to do so?
- What are your religious beliefs about life and death?
- How do you feel about ventilators, surgery, resuscitation, antibiotics, tube feeding, etc., if you become terminally ill or severely incapacitated?
- What if you become senile?
- What illness, disability, or treatment would be unacceptable?
- Do you want to receive artificial hydration and nutrition?
- What kind of medical treatment do you want if you had a condition that made you totally dependent on others for all of your care?
- Do you want to receive every treatment your doctor recommends? Do you trust your doctor's judgment?
- What diminished quality of life would be unacceptable to you?

WHAT SHOULD I DO IF I'M NOT COMFORTABLE TALKING ABOUT END-OF-LIFE ISSUES?

Talking about end-of-life issues can be difficult for anyone. However, it's up to you to take the initiative and express your wishes. Your family or loved ones are not likely to raise the issue for you.

It is so important to talk with your loved ones about your health care preferences. You may find it easier to talk with your doctor about your options so that you can make informed decisions.

Talking before a crisis can help you and your loved ones prepare for any difficult decisions related to health care at the end-of-life.

WHAT IS A LIVING WILL?

A Living Will is the most common type of Advance Directive. It outlines your wishes in writing and tells your doctor or health care provider, your wishes concerning end-of-life medical care. A Living Will pertains to artificial life support and is not implemented until a physician decides that the individual is terminal.

Basically, a Living Will is a document that allows you to decide whether or not to be kept on artificial life support. It can also include your decisions about organ donation or your wishes to die at home rather than in a hospital.

Remember, with a Living Will, you have to make all of these decisions while you are healthy and mentally competent to avoid any confusion about your true intent.

WHAT ARE THE LIMITATIONS OF LIVING WILLS?

Living Wills are limited in the range of treatment decisions they permit.

Living Wills do not apply in emergency situations.

For example, many serious events, such as strokes, Alzheimer's disease or comas, are not considered terminal diseases by many doctors and, therefore, may not be covered by Living Wills.

Or, for example, if you are seriously injured in a car accident, emergency personnel can do everything in their power to save your life.

You also should be aware that each state has different laws about Living Wills. Laws in some states are stricter than in others about when a Living Will can be used.

Most states limit the rights of pregnant patients to refuse certain treatments in order to protect the developing fetus.

Because of the limited applicability of Living Wills, you are encouraged to also have a Durable Power of Attorney for Health Care (DPAHC). (See page 63).

SHOULD I INCLUDE "AFTER DEATH" DECISIONS IN MY LIVING WILL?

Yes. You can help ease the burden on loved ones by making your wishes known. Things to consider include:

- Donating viable organs and tissue for transplant, research or medical education (or not). (See next page for more information.)
- Permit an autopsy for diagnostic and research purposes (or not).
- Preferences for burial or cremation.
- Preferences for funeral service and/or memorial service.

SIX THINGS YOU SHOULD KNOW ABOUT ORGAN AND TISSUE DONATION

Did you know?

- More than 68,000 patients are on the national organ transplant waiting list. Each day, at least 13 of them will die because the organs they need have not been donated.
- Organs you can donate: heart, kidneys, pancreas, lungs, liver, and intestines.
- Tissue you can donate: cornea, skin, bone marrow, heart valves, and connective tissue.
- To be transplanted, organs must receive blood until they are removed from the body of the donor. Therefore, it may be necessary to place the donor on a breathing machine temporarily or provide other organ-sustaining treatment.
- If you are old or seriously ill, you may not have organs or tissue suitable for transplant.
- The body of an organ donor can still be shown and buried after death.

TO WHOM SHOULD I GIVE COPIES OF MY LIVING WILL?

People generally give a copy to their physicians, health care advocate, family members, and other trusted individuals.

Remember, a Living Will is limited in the range of treatment decisions it permits. A Living Will pertains to artificial life support and is not implemented until a physician decides that the individual is terminal.

WHAT MAKES A LIVING WILL VALID?

In most states, there are four basic requirements that make a Living Will valid:

1. Age — you must be at least 18 years old to make a valid Living Will document.
2. Soundness of Mind — the person signing the Living Will cannot be mentally ill or mentally-disabled and must be acting of his or her own free will, without undue influence from others.
3. Witnesses — at least two people (we recommend three as some states require three witnesses) must watch you sign the Living Will.
4. Notary — your document should be notarized by a notary public. The notary public must observe you and your witnesses sign the document.

CAN ANYONE BE A WITNESS FOR MY LIVING WILL?

No! Do not use the following persons as a witness:

- Any person you appointed to make health care decisions on your behalf.
- Any person related to you by blood, marriage or adoption.
- Any person entitled to receive anything under any last will and testament that you have made.
- Your doctor or physician, or an employee of your doctor or physician.
- The operator or employee of a community care facility or residential care facility or residential care facility for the elderly.

IS A LIVING WILL APPLICABLE TO SOMEONE IN A PERSISTENT VEGETATIVE STATE?

In most states, the wishes expressed in a Living Will do not apply to someone in a persistent vegetative state (PVS).

PVS refers to an irreversible type of brain damage. Since the brain stem continues to support vital functions, such as respiration and circulation, they are not considered "terminal."

Because of the limited applicability of Living Wills, you are encouraged to also have a Durable Power of Attorney for Health Care.

WHAT IF I DO NOT MAKE A LIVING WILL AND I BECOME TERMINALLY ILL AND UNABLE TO MAKE DECISIONS REGARDING MY TREATMENT?

If you have no Living Will in this situation, your treatment decisions may be made, in front of a witness, by the attending doctors and any of the following persons, in the following order:

1. The person you designated in a Power of Attorney, if any.
2. Your court appointed guardian, if any. Your guardian must obtain court approval before making any decisions.
3. Your spouse.
4. Your adult child. However, if you have more than one child, then the decision is to be made by a majority of your available adult children.
5. Your parent or parents.
6. An adult brother or sister.

WHAT IS A DURABLE POWER OF ATTORNEY FOR HEALTH CARE (DPAHC)?

A Durable Power of Attorney for Health Care (DPAHC) is sometimes referred to as A Health Care (Medical) Power of Attorney.

It is a legal document that you can use to give someone permission to make medical decisions for you if you are unable to make those decisions yourself, temporarily or permanently. The person you name to represent you may be called an agent, health care proxy, patient advocate, or something similar, depending on where you live.

Unlike a Living Will, a DPAHC empowers some- one to act as that person's agent.

A DPAHC can be part of another Advance Directive form, such as a Health Care Directive or Living Will, or may be a separate document.

A DPAHC includes situations where you cannot make treatment decisions for yourself, but do not have a terminal condition.

DOES A DURABLE POWER OF ATTORNEY FOR HEALTH CARE HAVE TO BE IN WRITING?

Yes. The person you give the decision-making power to, is called the patient advocate. The patient advocate must sign an acceptance of responsibility statement before acting.

The patient advocate can make decisions for you only when you are unable to participate in medical treatment decisions. You may become temporarily or permanently unconscious from disease, accident or surgery. You may be awake but mentally unable to make decisions about your care due to disease or injury.

MUST I HAVE A DURABLE POWER OF ATTORNEY FOR HEALTH CARE BEFORE I CAN RECEIVE TREATMENT?

No. A health care provider cannot refuse care based on whether or not you have a Living Will or Durable Power of Attorney for Health Care.

However, without one or both of these Advance Directives you may receive a type of care you do not want. So it is important to prepare these documents now.

MUST I GIVE WRITTEN INSTRUCTIONS ABOUT MY TREATMENT?

No. Although you must name a patient advocate to act on your behalf, in writing; they do not need written instructions. It is always better for you, and easier for them, if they do have written instructions.

The advantage of written instructions is that everyone can read them and better understand your wishes.

WHAT SHOULD A DURABLE POWER OF ATTORNEY FOR HEALTH CARE INCLUDE?

At a minimum, it should include:

- Name, address and telephone number(s) of the person designated as the agent.
- A list of all powers the agent is to have.
- Guidelines and instructions for the agent to follow when exercising those powers.
- Other legal provisions, which may vary by state.

The main advantage of a Durable Power of Attorney for Health Care is that you can leave any medical instructions you wish. It should reflect your personal beliefs, whatever they may be.

WHICH IS BETTER: A LIVING WILL OR A DURABLE POWER OF ATTORNEY FOR HEALTH CARE?

In some states, laws make it better to have one, the other, or both. The decision is up to you.

But remember, a Living Will doesn't allow you to name someone to make your medical decisions, if that is what you want. Because of the limited applicability of Living Wills, it is often recommended that people also have medical powers of attorney.

It's a good idea to talk with your health care professional and/or attorney to determine what is best for you.

WHERE CAN I FIND ADVANCE DIRECTIVE FORMS AND INSTRUCTIONS?

You can get Advance Directive forms from:

- A local hospital.
- Long-Term Care Ombudsman program.
- Senior legal service or senior information and referral program, or a local/state medical society.
- Your physician will usually have forms appropriate for your state.
- Some medical centers offer classes in preparing Advance Directives.
- You can get state-specific directives from a lawyer or the public library.
- Your attorney.

WHAT IS A MEDICAL PROXY?

If a person becomes incompetent and does not have a medical durable power of attorney or guardian appointed by a court, the patient's family can choose a proxy (medical decision-maker) to speak on the person's behalf.

WHAT IS THE DIFFERENCE BETWEEN A MEDICAL PROXY AND A HEALTH CARE AGENT?

A health care agent is someone the individual has selected.

A proxy is chosen for a person by agreement of the family, or close friend. A proxy should be someone who has a close relationship with the patient and who knows that person's medical wishes.

If family and friends cannot decide who a proxy should be or, if they disagree with a proxy's decision, then they can object and petition the court to request guardianship (see page 21).

HOW DO I CHOOSE A HEALTH CARE AGENT?

There are several things to consider when selecting a health care agent. Make sure that person meets the legal criteria in your state for acting as an agent or proxy or representative. Consider the following:

- Would your agent be willing to speak on your behalf and be able to act on your wishes, even if they are really different from their own?
- Is it someone you trust with your life?
- Is it someone who knows you well and understands what is important to you?
- Would they be able to handle conflicting opinions from family members?
- Can they be a strong advocate with physicians and hospital personnel?
- Do they live near you, or are they willing to travel to be with you?

Keep in mind that potential advocates may be emotionally incapable of serving as your advocate. They may also later become unwilling or otherwise unable to serve due to death or disability.

TOPICS TO DISCUSS WITH YOUR HEALTH CARE AGENT

Choosing the best health care agent is important. Make sure he or she understands your wishes. Here are some questions to discuss with him or her:

- Which of the following do I most want to avoid near the end of my life: acute pain; being a financial burden to my family; being unable to think, or being unable to interact?
- If I was in a terminally ill condition and in extreme pain, would I want to be sedated near unconsciousness if it were necessary to control the pain?
- To avoid a fatal outcome, would you object to limbs being amputated if necessary to control the infection?
- Would you want medical treatment to prolong your life if you were confined to a nursing home permanently?
- What if you need someone to take care of you 24 hours a day?
- What if you no longer can recognize or interact with family or friends?
- What if you no longer can walk?
- What if you must spend all day in bed?
- What if you are in severe pain most of the time?
- What if you are on a feeding tube to keep you alive?
- What if you need a ventilator to keep you alive?

WHAT IS THE DEFINITION OF "TERMINALLY ILL"?

This usually refers to people who are close to death with no possible recovery.

It can also be defined as an incurable or irre-versible condition that without life-sustaining procedures, results in death within a relatively short time or a comatose state from which there can be no recovery.

WHAT IS LIFE-SUSTAINING TREATMENT?

"Life-sustaining treatment" may be defined as any medical procedure, device, or medication to keep an individual alive, (including major surgery or antibiotics). In most states, the law refers to a life-sustaining procedure as any medical procedure of treatment that meets both of the following requirements:

1. The use of mechanical or artificial means to sustain, restore or take the place of a spontaneous vital function, and which,
2. When applied to a patient in a terminal condition, would serve only to prolong the dying process.

In some states the law has been amended to include the withdrawal of nutrition and hydration as a life-sustaining procedure.

CAN MY HEALTH CARE AGENT OVERRIDE MY SPECIFIC ADVANCE DIRECTIVE INSTRUCTIONS?

No. Your health care agent cannot override your specific instructions in your Advance Directive.

Your health care surrogate must always act in your best interests and do his or her best to try to follow any and all of your health care wishes.

You will always be able to have control of your own medical care if you have an Advance Directive. But, if you are incompetent you will not be able to "change your mind" — so be careful in initial drafting.

WHAT IS A CPR DIRECTIVE?

CPR directives allow people to signal their refusal of cardiopulmonary resuscitation. There are two types of CPR directives:

1. Do Not Resuscitate (DNR): A patient in a hospital or nursing home may have a DNR order that limits the use of resuscitative measures if heartbeat or breathing stops. This should be communicated to the physician in a DPAHC.
2. Out-of-hospital CPR directive: Some states have statutes that allow an out-of-hospital CPR directive. This type of directive is used by a person who is in the terminal stages of an advanced illness who wants to ensure resuscitative measures are not used by paramedics or other rescue personnel.

In the hospital, DNR orders are part of your medical records and all medical professionals should be aware of them. For out-of-hospital occurrences, say in the home, a proscribed placard may need to be displayed, to ensure your wishes are adhered to. Check your state regulations.

In an emergency situation, EMS staff members do not have time to look for, or to evaluate different types of documentation. There is a possibility they may not acknowledge your directive, unless it is in plain sight.

PART 4

Estate Planning: Wills and Trusts

This section deals with essential will and trust documents. Many families have a lot of misconceptions about estate planning. Some think it's something only old people should do, while others think it's all about avoiding taxes, or it's only about money.

It is much more than these things. It's about who gets your possessions when you die.

Keep in mind that you should work with a lawyer and/or accountant who are knowledgeable about the laws in your state and experienced in issues concerning seniors.

WHAT IS AN ESTATE?

An estate consists of your assets: everything you own solely or jointly with someone else.

An estate can include money, property, and personal and/or business assets. It can also include IRA and investment accounts, promissory notes, money owed to you by others, personal items, and even intellectual property. It is the sum total of your property and money.

WHAT IS AN ESTATE PLAN?

It is an arrangement to distribute your assets according to your wishes after your death. Estate planning is different for everyone. At a minimum, your estate plan should start with a will. However, you may require much more. It is best to check with an attorney.

WHY SHOULD I PLAN MY ESTATE?

It is beneficial to plan your estate in order to:

- Manage your property during your lifetime.
- Ensure that your property passes to those persons or entities (charities) that you wish, in the way you wish.
- Partially or completely avoid probate.
- Realize any tax savings.
- Maximize the amount you pass on to your heirs.

In other words, it helps you control and manage after you die what you have accumulated during your lifetime. You worked hard to get what you have, so why should a judge or state law dictate what to do with your estate.

WHAT ARE SOME STRATEGIES THAT MAY BE USED FOR ESTATE PLANNING?

Strategies used for estate planning include:

- Joint tenancy with full rights of survivorship
- Wills
- Trusts
- Gifts

WHAT IS JOINT TENANCY WITH FULL RIGHTS OF SURVIVORSHIP?

This is one way that property can be held by more than one person. A joint owner cannot sell his or her interest without permission of all other owners. Upon the death of a joint owner, property automatically belongs to surviving owner(s) and provisions in a will do not affect it.

WHAT ARE THE ADVANTAGES TO HOLDING PROPERTY IN JOINT TENANCY WITH FULL RIGHTS OF SURVIVORSHIP?

Property held in joint tenancy does not go through probate: it passes directly to the surviving owner(s). Having property in joint tenancy may also reduce inheritance taxes.

The disadvantage is if the joint tenant is not your spouse. While it can save inheritance taxes, it can also result in increased federal estate taxes in certain circumstances.

Should you decide to sell an asset held jointly, you need the permission of each joint tenant and the spouse of each joint tenant. While it may be difficult to imagine, the possibility of future disagreement should be carefully considered.

Legal action can be used to break up a joint tenancy.

WHAT IS A WILL?

A will is a legal document that outlines your wishes for the disposition of your estate after your death.

Here are the basic elements generally included in a will:

- Your name and place of residence.
- A brief description of your assets.
- Names of spouse, children and other beneficiaries, such as charities or friends.
- Alternate beneficiaries, in the event a beneficiary dies before you do.
- Specific gifts, such as an auto or residence.
- Establishment of trusts, if desired.
- Cancellation of debts owed to you, if desired.
- Name of an executor (and contingent executor if first is unable or unwilling to serve) to manage the estate.
- Name of a guardian for minor children.
- Name of an alternative guardian, in the event your first choice is unable or unwilling to act.
- Your signature.
- Witnesses' signatures.

DO I NEED A WILL?

It's a good idea to have a will. Other than a properly set up living trust, there is no way for anyone to carry out your intended wishes for disposition of your possessions, without a will. If you don't spell out your wishes in a will, your state laws will dictate who gets what.

Even though writing a will may not be a very pleasant experience, don't kid yourself by making some of the following excuses:

- "I have already told everybody who gets what."
- "I don't have very much and nobody will want what I have."
- "I made a list of who gets what."

You would be surprised to know the number of families and friends torn apart by fighting over the distribution of one's money and possessions. In many cases, if you die without a will, someone (usually a family member) will be appointed by the court, to distribute your assets, according to state law (which may not be how you wish at all.)

HOW MUCH DOES IT COST TO HAVE AN ATTORNEY DRAFT A WILL?

Most attorneys will draft a simple will from a hundred dollars to a few hundred dollars, depending on how complicated your affairs are.

For a large estate it could cost several thousand dollars. But it's money well spent.

WHAT ARE THE BASIC LEGAL REQUIREMENTS FOR A WILL?

Keep in mind that wills may vary from state to state. What most wills have in common:

- A will should generally be typewritten or printed using a computer printer.
- The person making the will (testator) must be clearly identified in the will.
- The will should clearly state that this is your will and revoke all previously made wills.
- The testator must be at least 18 years old and of sound mind and body, at the time the will is made.
- The testator must sign and date the will.
- The testator's signature must generally be witnessed by at least two qualified individuals. Some states require three witness signatures.

WHAT IS A TESTATOR?

A testator is the person who makes a will. The identity of the testator is established at various points in the will.

WHAT IS THE DIFFERENCE BETWEEN A DECEDENT AND A TESTATOR?

The person who has died is referred to as the decedent. The maker or writer of a will is referred to as the testator.

WHO IS A BENEFICIARY?

A beneficiary is someone named to receive property or benefits in a will. In a trust, a beneficiary is a person who is to receive benefits from the trust.

ARE THERE DIFFERENT TYPES OF WILLS?

Yes. Each type is equally valid if done precisely in accordance with the law. It is recommended that you see a lawyer if you wish to draft a will.

Some of the most common types of wills are:

- Statutory Wills
- Holographic Wills
- Reciprocal Wills
- Joint Wills

WHAT IS A STATUTORY WILL?

It is a simple will written according to state law. You can get a form from your state legislator at no cost. All you have to do is fill in the blanks and sign it. But, you cannot cross out or change anything on the will. You can only use a statutory will in certain cases.

Most statutory wills allow you to:

- Leave up to two cash gifts of any amount to people or charities.
- Write a list of personal and household items and name the person or entity to receive them.
- Ensure that the rest of your property goes to your spouse. If he or she dies before you, the property is to be distributed equally among your children.
- Appoint a guardian and conservator in case you and your spouse both die before your children reach age 18.

HOW WOULD MY PROPERTY BE DIVIDED UNDER THE TERMS OF A STATUTORY WILL?

You may leave up to two cash gifts to people or charities. You could write a list, separate from your will, of personal and household items, naming whom you wished to receive each item.

All the rest of your property would go to your spouse. If your spouse died before you, all the property would be divided equally among your children.

ARE THERE REASONS NOT TO USE A STATUTORY WILL?

Yes. It is a good idea to consult with a lawyer to help write your will. A statutory will is insufficient if:

- You have substantial wealth and need tax planning for your estate.
- If you want to establish a trust fund.
- If you have assets outside the state.
- If you have a significant interest in a business or partnership.

WHAT IS A HOLOGRAPHIC WILL?

It is a do-it-yourself handwritten will. To be valid, this will must be totally in your own handwriting, signed and dated. In some states, if anything in the will is crossed out, the will becomes null and void. In other states, what is crossed out is certainly voided, but the rest may not be. About twenty states allow holographic wills, but it is best to have a more formal will.

A holographic will must be entirely written in the testator's handwriting and because it is believed to be self-authenticating, does not have to be witnessed to be valid.

However, holographic wills are highly prone to forgery, fraud, undue influence and other complications that lead to a contesting of the will. Probate judges also dislike seeing them because of the troubles they may cause.

WHAT IS A RECIPROCAL WILL?

A reciprocal will is used by married couples. With a reciprocal will, each spouse's will is a mirror image of the other. In most cases, a reciprocal will provides:

- Naming of an Executor. This is usually the spouse. It should also list an alternate.
- Payment of debts and taxes.
- Specific bequests of tangible property.
- Disposition of residual property.

A reciprocal will is not useful in larger estates, and can result in increased federal estate taxes upon the death of the surviving spouse.

USING A VALID WILL, CAN I BEQUEATH MY PROPERTY TO WHOMEVER I PLEASE?

Yes, with two exceptions. First, a spouse has certain rights in the estate, regardless of the provisions of the will. A spouse almost always has a choice of taking a share under the will, or taking a share set forth by law.

Secondly, a will does not affect property held in joint tenancy or life insurance policies with named beneficiaries.

CAN I GIVE MONEY TO GRANDCHILDREN BUT REQUIRE THEY SAVE IT?

Yes. You can establish a trust or custodial account, with grandchildren as beneficiaries. Money is given to each grandchild when he or she reaches the age you specify.

This is a great way to ensure that a grandchild has money for college, to start a business, or purchase a first house.

WHO CAN WITNESS A WILL?

A witness must be at least 18 years of age and competent. You shouldn't have anyone who is a beneficiary, witness your will.

Witnesses cannot sign outside each other's presence.

If someone contests the will, it is likely the will witnesses will be called to testify.

CAN I MAKE CHANGES TO MY WILL?

Yes. Since a will has no effect until you die, you can change it any time during your life. You can either attach an amendment to the old will, known as a codicil, or have an entirely new will drafted by a lawyer.

If you sign a new will, destroy all the copies of the old one.

CAN WILLS BE CONTESTED?

Yes, and usually on one of the following grounds:

- Incompetence of the writer of the will.
- Undue Influence.
- Improper execution.

Some testators (writer of the will) insert a "no-contest clause" to automatically exclude anyone who challenges the will in court.

Renouncing of a will by a spouse is called the "right of election." The surviving spouse can elect to take a share of the estate that is spelled out by the state (sometimes called elective share or statutory share), rather than accept whatever inheritance the will specifies (if any). Paperwork must be filed with the court, usually during the probate process.

The elective share protects a surviving spouse from accidentally or deliberately being written out of the will.

WHAT IS A JOINT WILL?

A joint will is made in conjunction with another's will and requires distribution of property in a certain way regardless of who dies first.

For example, with a married couple, when one dies, the joint will can't be changed by the survivor without risking a will contest in court.

It is not advisable to have a joint will for larger estates.

WHAT IS AN ETHICAL WILL?

An ethical will is distinct from a legal will in that it is focused on conveying the writer's values and principals to the next generation.

An ethical will is a way to pass on your beliefs and values, life lessons, hopes and dreams, love, and forgiveness.

Many ethical wills are written as last letters to loved ones before going into battle or prior to particularly risky surgeries. Some ethical wills are preserved on video or CD-ROM.

WHAT IS INTESTACY?

"Intestacy" is a legal term for your estate if you die without a will.

If that happens, the court will distribute your estate according to the rules of intestate succession. Basically, the state statutes will determine who your heirs are and how much of a share in your estate they are entitled to inherit.

A recent Gallup Poll found that half of American adults do not have a will.

WHAT IF I DIE WITHOUT A WILL?

With few exceptions, your things will be distributed according to state law, sometimes called intestate succession rules.

Check with an attorney about the laws in your state. In most states, if you die without a written will, usually, your spouse and children receive your property first; if you aren't survived by a spouse or children, your grandchildren might be next in line, followed by your parents, siblings, nieces and nephews, and cousins. If you die without any relatives, your assets will pass to the state.

WHAT IS A TRUST?

A trust is a legal agreement that arranges for another person, bank or trust company to manage or control your property for your beneficiaries.

When you sign a trust agreement, it only creates the trust. You then have to transfer property into the trust in order for it to be funded (have property in it). If you wish, you can name yourself as beneficiary and as your own trustee.

Purposes of a trust include controlling assets after death, avoiding probate, providing for disability, and reducing taxes.

WHAT IS A TRUST ESTATE AND A TRUST AGREEMENT?

The trust estate is all the property owned by a trust.

A trust agreement is an agreement establishing and setting forth the material terms of a trust.

WHO IS A TRUSTEE?

A "Trustee" is a party who is given legal responsibility to hold property in the best interest of, or "for the benefit of another."

The Trustee is one placed in a position of responsibility for another, a responsibility enforceable in a court of law.

A Trustee is a person(s) or institution responsible for the administration of a trust.

WHAT DOES SUCCESSOR TRUSTEE MEAN?

A "Successor Trustee" is the person or institution who takes over the management of trust property when the original Trustee has died or becomes incapacitated.

WHO SHOULD HAVE A TRUST?

You should discuss the advantages of a trust over a will (even with a will creating a "testamentary trust") with an attorney if:

- You are the parent of minor children.
- Privacy is important to you, your business or your family.
- You own real property, particularly any property outside of your home state.
- Your estate has a gross value in excess of $1,000,000 (this amount increases slowly to $3.5 million in 2009; the tax is completely repealed in 2010, but reinstated in 2011).
- You wish to avoid conservatorship or probate.

A trust in NOT necessary for everyone, and some lawyers prefer to have matters go through probate, while others wish to have their clients avoid probate entirely. It certainly makes sense to discuss it with your lawyer.

WHAT IS A TESTAMENTARY TRUST?

A will can have a trust written into it. It is called a "testamentary trust". It is set into motion by the Court after the will reaches a certain point of execution, and is used only after the death of the person whose estate it represents.

The testamentary trust is often created so that inheritance does not go directly to the beneficiary. It is often used to prevent children from receiving large sums of money before they are mature enough to properly manage it.

Trusts are also created for charitable organizations or care of pets upon the death of the testator.

WHAT IS A LIVING TRUST?

A "living trust", also known as, *inter vivos*, is a trust that allows a person to put his assets into a trust which is managed according to instructions given by the person creating the trust. This is done for the benefit of named beneficiaries, including the creator of the trust.

A living trust avoids probate and therefore gets assets distributed significantly more quickly than a will does. It also offers a higher level of confidentiality, as probate proceedings are a matter of public record.

Additionally, trusts are usually harder to contest than wills. On the downside, a living trust takes longer to put together than a will, and requires more ongoing maintenance.

Although both a will and a living trust can be modified or revoked at any time before death, such changes are slightly more time-consuming for a living trust. Additionally, assets that a person wants to move to a living trust, such as real estate and bank or brokerage accounts, have to be re-titled. (By contrast, a testamentary trust receives property only after you die.)

A living trust can be revocable or irrevocable.

DO I NEED A LIVING TRUST IF I ALREADY HAVE A WILL?

Maybe. Many people falsely believe that having a will avoids probate. Not necessarily.

When you die the courts utilize probate to approve or disapprove your will, and to supervise the disposition of your assets according to your will and state law. Having a will is an important part of an estate plan, however, it is not a complete plan.

Talk this over with your attorney or financial planner.

WHAT IS A REVOCABLE LIVING TRUST?

A "revocable living trust" is a document stating who controls your assets while you are alive and what will happen to those assets when you die.

It is a trust in which any of its provisions can be changed, or the trust itself can be canceled at any time by the grantor. A grantor is the person who transfers assets into a trust for the benefit of another.

A revocable trust is a legal entity that can hold title to property in the same manner as other legal entities, such as partnerships and corporations, except that title is in the name of the trustee. As such, it avoids probate by having title in the name of the trustee of the revocable trust and not the decedent at the time of death.

At that time, the named trustee, or successor trustee, has authority to pay the decedent's bills and has a fiduciary responsibility to distribute the trust properly to beneficiaries as provided in the provisions of the trust. A revocable trust is the only device that can be used with all types of property and does not depend upon survival of specific persons to avoid probate.

HOW IS A REVOCABLE LIVING TRUST DIFFERENT FROM A WILL?

If you set up a living trust, you are the creator or grantor, because you are transferring property to the trust, which in turn will distribute the property to the beneficiaries, after your death.

You are also most likely the trustee, which means that you administer the property and, following the trust instrument's provisions, distribute the income from the property or the property itself to the beneficiaries.

While you are alive, you can be the grantor, trustee, and beneficiary.

After you die, if you have been the sole trustee, the successor trustee takes over the trust administration and can sell your assets and distribute the proceeds to the beneficiaries. If your young children are the beneficiaries, the successor trustee can distribute income from the trust to pay for their upbringing and education.

HOW IS A REVOCABLE LIVING TRUST DIFFERENT FROM A WILL?, CONT.

If this sounds exactly like what you can do under a will, you're absolutely right. The difference is that you have set this up carefully during your lifetime and, because the trust owns your property, there is no transfer of ownership after your death, as is the case with the will process. So your beneficiaries receive the property promptly, rather than having to wait for a will to wind its way through a year or so of probate court, with its attendant costs.

WHAT IS AN IRREVOCABLE TRUST?

An "irrevocable trust" is a permanent trust.
Once you create it, it cannot be revoked,
amended or changed in any way.

For instance, the grantor may set up a trust
under which he or she will receive income
earned on the trust property, but that bars
access to the trust principal.

ADVANTAGES OF A REVOCABLE TRUST

Revocable trusts (sometimes called "living trusts") have the following advantages over wills:

- Privacy. With revocable trusts, financial affairs and to whom property is given at death are private. Wills and inventories of probate estate are matters of public record.
- Cost Savings. Assets named in a revocable trust avoid the probate costs and additional attorney fees that would be incurred in a probate estate (although varying from state to state, accounting and attorney's fees and other administration costs can average perhaps three to four percent in a probate estate versus one to two percent in non-probate estates). This is particularly beneficial if real estate is located in a state other than the state of residence. Probate would otherwise be required in more than one state.
- Convenience. Revocable trusts serve as a conservatorship substitute in the event of incapacity (although use of durable powers of attorney usually can achieve much the same result).
- Coordination of Estate Plan. A revocable trust coordinates the entire estate plan and all assets through one instrument, thereby avoiding property going to beneficiaries in disproportionate amounts through joint tenancy or beneficiary designations.

ADVANTAGES OF A REVOCABLE TRUST, CONT.

- Continuity. Revocable trusts serve as an ongoing mechanism after death to pay bills, pay taxes, and manage and distribute assets without any delay (although delays solely attributable to the probate process are normally inconsequential in a well managed estate) or the court approval necessitated by probate proceedings.
- Stability. Revocable trusts normally do not need to be changed due to moving to another state.
- Security. Due to the lesser degree of formality surrounding their execution and the lack of an existing court proceeding in which to make an objection, revocable trusts are somewhat more difficult (and thus usually less likely) to be legally challenged after death.

The one creating a revocable trust retains complete control over the assets of the revocable trust during their lifetime and can change its provisions at any time in the same manner as a will. All income from trust assets would continue to be shown on the grantor's individual tax return (Form 1040) and no trust income tax return needs to be filed as long as the grantor is serving as a trustee. If at any time the grantor is not serving as a trustee, an information return would be filed showing the income as taxed to the grantor.

DISADVANTAGES OF REVOCABLE TRUST

Some of the disadvantages of a revocable trust include:

- Greater Initial Cost and Effort. There is a greater initial cost and effort in drafting and titling assets (trust funding) in a revocable trust compared to a will. The trust-funding process does have a desirable side benefit, however, as it frequently uncovers title errors before they become a problem and at a time when they are easier to correct.
- Probate Avoidance Not Assured. The grantor must be careful to place all subsequently acquired titled assets in the trust or probate may still be necessary.
- Possible Income Tax Detriments. There are some normally minor income tax detriments that may be incurred during the one or two year period of trust administration following death that would not be present if a will were used for estate planning.

DO I NEED A TRUST TO AVOID PROBATE?

Again, state laws vary. Consult with an attorney or certified financial planner. Generally, avoiding probate in estate planning allows the distribution of the property of testators to the person they wish to have it at a time they so desire without incurring a substantial amount of income, estate and inheritance taxes as well as attorney's fees and other administrative costs.

CAN I AVOID PROBATE?

There are three common estate-planning tools that can be used to avoid probate in the distribution of testators' property at death:

- Joint tenancy with rights of survivorship.
- Beneficiary designations.
- Revocable trusts.

Joint tenancy is applicable to all property types except retirement plans and individual retirement accounts (IRAs). Beneficiary designations can be used for life insurance policies, retirement plans and individual retirement accounts. Revocable trusts can be utilized, unlike the first two devices, with all types of property.

Seek advice from an attorney.

WHAT IS THE COST OF A REVOCABLE LIVING TRUST?

The exact cost of a revocable living trust depends on how valuable and complicated your assets are, whether standard documents can be used, how many assets must be transferred to the trustee, and whether tax planning is needed. Before you ask an attorney to set up a trust for you, ask for estimates of how much it will cost, how much writing a will would cost, and how much probating your estate would cost. The fee arrangement should be in writing.

If you do not plan to serve as trustee, you should consider any fees you might have to pay the trustee and whether those fees would replace fees you are already paying to manage your assets.

A standard revocable living trust package should include:

- Trust document.
- The transfer of assets to the trust.
- A "pour-over" will to add other assets to the trust.
- A similar durable power of attorney.
- It also might include descriptive materials and related legal documents, such as a directive to physicians or "Living Will."

WHAT IS "FUNDING" THE TRUST?

For a living trust to take effect, title to the grantor's assets must be transferred into the trust. For example, title to any bank accounts, stock certificates or real estate owned by the grantor must be transferred into the trust.

Contrary to the impression created by many living trust salespeople, the grantor must take affirmative steps to transfer assets and fund the trust. Merely executing the living trust itself will not cause the trust to become funded.

WILL A REVOCABLE LIVING TRUST HELP ME WITH ESTATE TAXES?

With proper planning, a living trust can be a valuable estate and tax planning device. However, there is no inherent estate tax advantage to using a living trust. While a trust may contain provisions taking effect at death which do save on taxes, the identical tax savings can be contained in the grantor's will instead of a living trust.

Sometimes a revocable living trust is set up in order to avoid probate.

WHAT IS A GIFT?

Gifts are a common way for people to shrink their estates to minimize taxes.

You can give up to $11,000 per year to any number of individuals without paying gift taxes. You can make tax-free gifts in excess of $11,000 to an individual if the additional money is paid, on behalf of this other person, directly to an institution for medical care or education.

WHAT IS THE RESIDUARY ESTATE?

The residuary estate is the portion of a decedent's estate that is left after the payment of specific legacies, debts, and estate administration expenses.

When beneficiaries are nominated to inherit the residuary estate, they get everything that is left after specific legacies, debts, and estate expenses.

For example, you could name one person to receive 75 percent and another to receive 25 percent (or any other percentage). There is not a limit on how many people you may list. You may even include a charity.

WHAT IS THE DIFFERENCE BETWEEN A SPECIFIC BENEFICIARY AND A RESIDUARY BENEFICIARY?

The specific beneficiary gets just the gift you name. The residuary beneficiary gets what is left after the Executor distributes the "specific gifts" and estate debts.

WHO ISSUES THE DEATH CERTIFICATE?

Usually the death certificate is issued by a government agency such as the local health department. In most cases, the funeral director can help you obtain a certified death certificate for the decedent. The person filing for probate will need multiple certified copies of the death certificate.

As soon as a copy of the death certificate is received, be sure to read it carefully. If there are any typos or erroneous information it is better to correct it sooner rather than later. The information is recorded into official records and could cause a delay in benefit payments, etc.

WHAT IS AN EXECUTOR?

The executor is a person appointed by a testator (the person who died) to carry out the terms of the will.

An administrator is the person appointed by a court to represent an estate when no will was provided or the will doesn't name an executor. In some states this person is referred to as a personal representative.

HOW DO I SELECT AN EXECUTOR?

First, you need to think about who is best suited to handle your estate when you are no longer around. This key person (or organization) should have your complete trust when it comes to administering your estate and distributing your assets to your beneficiaries.

In most cases, it helps to choose someone who is organized, who gets along with family members, and someone who will accept the job.

You can choose almost anyone who is legally competent to serve as executor — such as your spouse, sibling, friend, business associate, financial or legal advisor. You can also name a corporate executor, such as a bank trust department.

ARE THERE RULES ABOUT WHO CAN BE MY EXECUTOR?

The person you choose to be your executor must be 18 or older (depending on the state), and legally competent.

Some states require the executor to be a resident of the same state, or a relative.

Most people choose a relative or close friend as executor. If your estate is large or complicated you may wish to appoint a trust company to act as your executor.

WHAT ARE THE DUTIES OF AN EXECUTOR?

State probate laws vary, but here are the basic duties in most states:

- Collect and provide safekeeping for the estate's assets.
- Notify creditors and pay all valid debts.
- Collect any sums owed the estate.
- File claims for pension and profit-sharing plan benefits, Social Security benefits, and Veterans' benefits.
- Manage the estate's assets.
- Sell assets, as directed by the Will or required by state law, to pay estate expenses or legacies.
- Keep detailed records of all estate transactions and submit records to beneficiaries and/or the probate court.
- Distribute assets to beneficiaries.
- File the decedent's final federal income-tax return.
- Choose a tax year for the estate.
- File the estate's income-tax returns.
- File state death-tax returns.
- Complete and file the federal estate tax return.
- Most executors arrange your funeral.

SHOULD I ASK THE PERSON I NAME AS MY EXECUTOR TO ACCEPT THE POSITION?

Yes! You should always discuss the role with the person in advance so that the person you choose knows what is involved with the job. Remember, the person you name in your will as executor is not obligated to act as your executor.

It's a good idea to name an alternate, too.

DOES THE EXECUTOR GET PAID?

Your executor has the right to be paid for his or her services. However, family members may agree to administer the estate without taking a fee. If you did not make any provision for payment in your will, your executor can apply to the Probate Court for a reasonable fee.

There are two reasons why you should make arrangements to pay your executor:

1. You clearly authorize your executor to pay himself or herself.
2. You set a maximum limit on how much your executor may take.

If you have more than one executor, they will have to share the fees, whether they are set by the Court or stipulated in your will. Fees received by executors are taxable in their hands.

If you appoint professionals, such as lawyers, accountants or a trust company as your executor, they will expect to be paid for their services. You should work out in advance whether the professional executor is to be entitled to an executor's fee instead of the professional's ordinary charges or in addition to such charges.

SHOULD I CHOOSE A BACK-UP EXECUTOR?

Yes. You should appoint an alternate to replace your executor in case your first choice is unwilling or unable to act as executor at your death. Even if you have chosen your spouse to be your executor it is a good idea to choose an alternate.

If your executor is unable to act and you have not named an alternate in your will, the Probate Court will appoint one. The court-appointed replacement is called an administrator.

The Court generally chooses a member of your family and this person exercises all the powers you conferred upon your executor in your will. Nevertheless, the person appointed by the Court may not be someone you would have chosen to administer your estate.

IS THE EXECUTOR/PERSONAL REPRESENTATIVE RESPONSIBLE FOR DEBTS OF THE DECEASED?

Generally, debts are paid from assets in the estate. The Executor/Personal Representative is only responsible if careless.

For instance, an executor/personal representative might be liable if he or she distributes estate assets to beneficiaries before proper debts are paid.

A short will often used with a living trust (see page 114) stating that any property left out of the living trust will become part of (or "pour over", into) the living trust upon death.

WHAT IS PROBATE?

It is a legal process that the courts use to transfer title to property and make sure your debts are paid after you die. This process happens whether you die with a will or without one.

The probate process makes sure that your creditors are paid and that any taxes due on your estate are paid BEFORE assets are distributed to your family or friends.

IS PROBATE BAD?

Hmmm, that's a good question. Probate certainly is an orderly process for paying your debts and passing your assets to your heirs. That's a good thing.

In many cases, probate can be expensive and take a long time. During this time all assets are frozen and the beneficiaries generally get nothing. That doesn't sound good, does it?

Remember, if there are probate assets, with or without a will, probate is necessary. However, if all property was held jointly with a spouse and the spouse survived, or a good trust was set up, there would be no probate of an estate.

One of the biggest drawbacks is that probate is expensive. The money used for probate may come directly from your estate or your heirs.

DOES HAVING A WILL AVOID PROBATE PROCEDURES?

No. The issue of whether probate procedures must be followed is not solely dependent on whether or not you have a will.

If there is a will, the initial purpose of probate is to prove its validity. The person named in the will as personal representative/executor is then appointed to proceed with administering the estate.

WHAT IS THE PROCESS OF PROBATE?

The probate process starts in the county of the decedent's legal residence at death. The probate court is located in the county courthouse. Even though the probate process varies slightly from state to state, there are three basic steps required in most states:

1. Someone must take inventory and manage the decedent's estate.
2. The decedent's lawful debts and taxes must be paid.
3. Whatever is left of the decedent's probate estate must be distributed according to the decedent's will, or, if there is no will, according to state law.

If someone dies without a will, the probate court will appoint an administrator to handle the probate matters. If there is a will, the executor usually handles the probate matters.

IS THERE MORE THAN ONE METHOD TO PROBATE AN ESTATE?

Yes. There are several procedures for smaller estates. Some states have what they think are "simplified procedures" to handle certain estates whose value is below certain dollar limits. The limits may be as low as $5,000 or as high as $100,000, depending on the state.

Whether the simplified procedure is available or even appropriate given the particular circumstances is something that a lawyer can discuss with you. For example, if there are debts against the estate, it may make sense to go through regular probate processes.

For larger estates, you can specify in your will a preference for either independent or supervised probate.

In independent probate there are no formal court hearings. The estate still must be kept open for at least five months to allow creditors to submit claims.

HOW DOES ONE INITIATE THE PROBATE PROCESS?

The filing of the Petition for Probate Will and Appointment of Executor (or, depending on the state, something similar) with the court, begins the probate process.

This document includes basic information about the decedent, such as, social security number, date of death, next of kin. Some courthouses have a pre-printed form that you can fill out.

More than likely there will be some fees associated with the filing of a Petition for Probate of Will and Appointment of Executor. There may be a filing fee and administrative fees that may include a newspaper legal notice announcing the probate to potential creditors.

The petition can be brought by a surviving spouse, a child, an heir, or the personal representative of the decedent. A creditor may petition for probate if no petition is filed within 30 days of the person's death.

The person filing for probate will also need to obtain multiple certified copies of the death certificate, with raised seal.

WHAT SHOULD I KNOW ABOUT PROBATE AND TAXES?

A lot of people seem to be confused about this topic. Avoiding probate does NOT mean avoiding taxes. It is possible to have an estate that avoids the probate process but is still subject to estate taxes.

Remember, the probate process does not generate any revenues to either the state or federal government in the form of taxes. Instead, probate is the legal process in each state by which property that was in the decedent's name can pass to his beneficiaries and heirs after the debts and expenses have been paid.

Estate taxes, on the other hand, are a totally different matter. Estate taxes are based on ownership, control, and enjoyment of property, regardless of whether or not that particular item of property was or was not probated.

It is important that you speak with a lawyer or certified financial advisor to understand the differences between the legal consequences of ownership and the tax consequences of ownership.

WHAT PROPERTY IS NOT SUBJECT TO PROBATE PROCEDURES?

There is some property that is not subject to probate procedures. Property such as money held in a joint bank account, real estate (if your spouse's name or joint tenant's name is on the deed) and life insurance benefits, if a person living at the time of your death was named as beneficiary in the policy.

HOW LONG DOES IT TAKE TO PROBATE AN ESTATE?

The time depends, among many factors: on the size of the estate, whether there is a surviving spouse and whether the validity of the will is questioned.

WHAT COSTS ARE INVOLVED IN PROBATING AN ESTATE?

The Executor/Personal Representative may charge a fee. If the Executor/Personal Representative seeks legal counsel, there will be attorney fees. In most states, a filing fee and an inventory fee (based on the value of the probate estate) must be paid to probate court.

Fees are paid by the Executor/Personal Representative from assets of the estate.

WHAT IS THE ESTATE TAX?

According to the IRS, the Estate Tax is a tax on your right to transfer property at your death. It consists of an accounting of everything you own or have certain interests in at the date of death. The fair market value of these items is used, not necessarily what you paid for them or what their values were when you acquired them. The total of all these items is your "Gross Estate." The includible property may consist of cash and securities, real estate, insurance, trusts, annuities, business interests and other assets.

Once you have accounted for the Gross Estate, certain deductions are allowed in arriving at your "Taxable Estate".

After the net amount is computed, the value of lifetime taxable gifts (beginning with gifts made in 1977) is added to this number and the tax is computed. The tax is then reduced by the available unified credit. Presently, the amount of this credit reduces the computed tax so that only total taxable estates and lifetime gifts that exceed $1,000,000 will actually have to pay tax.

WHAT IS A SUPPLEMENTAL NEEDS TRUST?

The purpose of a Supplemental Needs Trust is to enable the grantor to provide for the continuing care of a disabled spouse, child, relative or friend. The beneficiary of a well-drafted Supplemental Needs Trust will have access to the trust assets for purposes other than those provided by public benefits programs. In this way, the beneficiary will not lose eligibility for benefits such as Supplemental Security Income, Medicaid and low-income housing.

An alternative may be long term care insurance.

HOW DO I FIND A GOOD WILL AND TRUST ATTORNEY?

Tips to consider when shopping for an attorney:

- Ask friends if they know someone who specializes in estate planning.
- Ask other professionals you trust: your accountant, doctor, clergy, etc.
- Contact the local bar association and ask for a referral.
- Don't pick a lawyer from the phone book or general advertising.
- Interview several attorneys before you pick one.

HOW OFTEN SHOULD I UPDATE MY WILL AND/OR TRUST?

It is always a good idea to review your will and/or trust at least once a year. Also, review your will or trust if:

- Life changing events occur.
- Death of your spouse.
- Birth of children, grandchildren.
- Shifts in asset values.

WHERE SHOULD I KEEP MY WILL?

Store your will safely. You should keep your will some place other than a safe deposit box.

Tell only your nominated executor where you keep it. You may also wish to give the executor a copy or a second original.

You can store it at home but you should consider the following points:

- A will can be easily lost, as sometimes happens when people move.
- There is also the added question of security: do you want other members of your family to have access to your will?

WHAT IS A LETTER OF INSTRUCTION?

It is an informal, non-binding, non-legal document, that explains any personal matters not mentioned in the will. Things it might include:

- How furniture, jewelry, photos, or letters are to be divided.
- Computer passwords.
- Inventory and/or appraisal of all personal belongings.
- Special instructions for pet care.
- Explanations or instructions regarding investments, rental property, etc.

PART 5

Funerals and Cremations

Every culture has its own customs on how to deal with death. The United States of America, as a melting pot of cultures, has every imaginable option available to you. What you choose will be dictated by your own beliefs and desires. This section helps you plan for these final steps in the cycle of life.

WHAT IS THE IMPORTANCE OF A FUNERAL?

Funerals and memorial services are valuable rituals. The funeral is a ceremony of proven worth and value for those who mourn. It provides an opportunity for the survivors and others who share in the loss to express their love, respect, grief and appreciation for a life that has been lived.

It is a time to honor a beloved life.

It permits facing openly and realistically the crisis that death presents. Through the funeral, the bereaved take that first step toward emotional adjustment to their loss and healing.

SHOULD I PRE-PLAN MY OWN FUNERAL?

That decision is totally up to you. Typically when a loved one dies, family members and friends are confronted with many decisions about the funeral, all of which must be made quickly and often under a great deal of emotional duress.

Some people see funeral planning as an extension of will and estate planning. Often it brings a "peace of mind" by not burdening others with unfinished business.

Some people think it is enough to write down their wishes. Others prefer to write down their wishes and have some form of financing in place to carry out those wishes.

Planning ahead does not have to mean paying ahead, but it can save money.

TEN THINGS EVERYONE SHOULD KNOW ABOUT PLANNING A FUNERAL OR CREMATION SERVICE

1. Funeral or cremation service arrangements need to be documented. Put it in writing. Share your wishes with several people you can trust — family members, friends, funeral counselor.
2. Find out what government benefits are available. Check with the Social Security office (www.ssa.gov) and the Department of Veterans Affairs (www.cem.va.gov/benvba.htm).
3. Decide the final disposition — burial, mausoleum or cremation.
4. Be informed about the choices available.
5. Incorporate the wishes of family members if appropriate. Prearranging is a good way to discuss and resolve any issues.
6. If you are planning on applying for Medicaid assistance, a prearranged funeral agreement can be beneficial. In some states, a prearranged funeral or cremation service may be treated as an exempt asset for Medicaid qualification purposes. Check with an attorney.

160

7. Don't be afraid to ask about prices. The costs vary considerably from company to company.
8. Even if your insurance provides a lump sum benefit, it may not be enough to cover all costs.
9. Consider planning and prepaying your arrangements.
10. Talk with a local funeral counselor.

HOW DO I START PRE-PLANNING MY FUNERAL?

Before you can make funeral plans you need to be aware of the choices available.

First, you have to decide on one of the following:

- Body donation
- Burial
- Cremation

You can make arrangements directly with a funeral establishment or through a funeral planning or memorial society — a nonprofit organization that provides information about funerals but doesn't offer funeral services.

HOW DO I CHOOSE A FUNERAL PROVIDER?

You may not realize that you do not have to use a funeral home or mortuary to plan and conduct a funeral. You are not legally required to do so.

However, most of us are not familiar with many of the details and legal requirements involved in burying someone. In most cases it is wise to use the services of a professional.

Some people select a funeral provider or mortuary because it is close to home or the family has used their services previously. Some people select a provider based on a referral from a friend. Some people shop around for the best price.

SHOULD I PRE-PAY FOR MY FUNERAL ARRANGEMENTS?

If you are thinking about prepaying for funeral goods and services consider these issues before putting down any money:

- Are you protected if the company goes out of business?
- What are you paying for — only merchandise, such as a casket and vault, or are you buying the funeral service as well?
- What happens to the money you have pre-paid? Is it in a trust? States have different requirements for handling funds paid for prearranged funeral services.
- What happens to interest income that is prepaid and put into a trust account?
- Can you cancel the contract and get a full refund if you change your mind?
- Can you transfer the plan to another funeral home if you move out of state?

If you do pre-pay, make sure that your family members are informed so they don't end up paying for the same arrangements.

WHAT IS A FUNERAL PROVIDER?

According to the Federal Trade Commission (FTC), you are a funeral provider if you sell or offer to sell both funeral goods and funeral services to the public.

You do not have to be a licensed funeral director and your business does not have to be a licensed funeral home to be covered by the Funeral Rule (see page 166). Cemeteries, crematories, and other businesses can also be "funeral providers" if they market both funeral goods and services.

You must comply with the Rule even if a particular consumer buys only goods or only funeral services, but not both. If you offer to sell both goods and services, you must comply with the Rule for every customer. However, you are not covered by the Rule if you sell only funeral goods, such as caskets, but not services relating to the disposition of remains.

Funeral goods are all products sold directly to the public in connection with funeral services.

Funeral services are:

- Services used to care for and prepare bodies for burial, cremation, or other final disposition.
- Services used to arrange, supervise, or conduct the funeral ceremony or final disposition of human remains.

165

WHAT IS THE FUNERAL RULE?

The Funeral Rule requires funeral directors to give you itemized prices in person and, if you ask, over the phone. The Rule also requires funeral directors to give you information about their goods and services.

Some funeral providers offer various packages of commonly selected goods and services that make up a funeral. However, you have the right to select individual items.

The FTC has oversight responsibilities for The Funeral Rule.

DO FUNERAL DIRECTORS TAKE ADVANTAGE OF THE BEREAVED?

Most funeral providers are caring individuals who help people deal with a very stressful time. They serve the same families 80% of the time, and many have spent most of their lives in the same community. If they took advantage of bereaved families, they could not stay in business. The fact that the average funeral home has been in business over 59 years shows that most funeral directors respect the wishes of the bereaved families.

Most funeral providers look upon their profession as a service, but it is also a business. Like any business, funeral homes must make a profit to exist. As long as the profit is reasonable and the services rendered are necessary, complete, and satisfactory to the family, profit is legitimate.

FIVE BENEFITS OF THE FUNERAL RULE

When you talk with a funeral counselor, keep these things in mind:

- You have the right to choose the funeral goods and services you want (with a few exceptions).
- The funeral provider must state this right in writing on the general price list.
- If state or local law requires you to buy a particular item, the funeral provider must disclose it on the price list, with a reference to the specific law.
- The funeral provider may not refuse, or change a fee, to handle a casket you bought elsewhere.
- A funeral provider that offers cremations must make alternative containers available.

WHAT ARE THE BASIC FUNERAL COSTS?

Keep in mind that funeral costs can vary greatly from one provider to another. Some of the basic costs include:

- Basic services fee for the funeral director and staff (usually for securing necessary permits and copies of death certificate, preparing the notices, sheltering the remains, coordinating arrangements with a cemetery, crematory or other third parties).
- Charges for other services and merchandise, embalming and other preparation, use of funeral home for viewing, ceremony or memorial service, use of grave-side equipment, use of hearse or limousine, casket, vault, or other container; and cremation or internment.
- Cash advances for buying flowers, obituary notices, pallbearers, officiating clergy, organists and soloists.

WHAT IS THE BEST KIND OF
FUNERAL TO HAVE?

There is no "best" kind of funeral. Because every family is different, not everyone wants the same type of funeral.

Ultimately, this is a personal decision and should be made by you. It is also a good idea to give some consideration to the needs of your family and friends as well.

Funeral practices are often influenced by traditions both religious and cultural. Sometimes costs or personal preferences are the deciding factors. Your funeral could be simple or elaborate, private or public, religious or secular. You get to decide if the body will be present at the funeral, if there will be a viewing or visitation, and if so, if the casket will be open or closed, and whether the remains will be buried or cremated. You may decide you don't want a funeral at all.

WHAT ARE THE THREE MOST BASIC FUNERALS?

In the United States, the three most basic funerals are:

1. Traditional, full service — This type usually includes a viewing or visitation and formal funeral service, use of a hearse to transport the body to the funeral site and cemetery, and burial. (This is also generally the most expensive type of funeral.)
2. Direct Burial — The body is buried shortly after death, usually in a simple container. There is no viewing, visitation, or embalming. Sometimes a memorial service is held at the grave site at a later date.
3. Direct Cremation — The body is cremated shortly after death, without embalming. The cremated remains are put in an urn or container.

HOW MUCH DOES THE AVERAGE FUNERAL COST?

Prices vary greatly from one provider to another. Average funeral and burial expenses range from $6000 to $10,000. The prices below reflect a national price range at the time of writing this book.

Service	Approximate Cost
Services of the funeral director	$1200–$2500
Casket	$600–$8500
Urn	$125–$7000
Mausoleum	$1500+
Grave Liner	$50–$3000
Burial Vault	$500–$9000
Memorial Marker	$750–$10,000
Opening and closing the grave	$400–$1500
Embalming	$150–$550
Cremation	$500–$2500
Grave Site	$750–$3000

WHO PAYS FOR FUNERALS FOR THE INDIGENT?

Other than the family, there are veteran, union, and other organizational benefits to pay for funerals, including, in certain instances, a lump sum death payment from Social Security. In most states, some form of public aid allowance is available from the state, county, or city or a combination.

Most funeral directors are aware of the various benefits and know how to obtain them for the indigent. However, funeral directors often absorb the costs.

WHY WILL I NEED MULTIPLE COPIES OF THE DEATH CERTIFICATE?

Each state requires a death certificate before a burial or cremation takes place.

It will be necessary to notify various business and governmental agencies that death has occurred. You may need a death certificate for:

- Probate court
- Real estate transfers
- Motor vehicle transfers
- Banks, brokers, investments
- Veterans affairs
- Social security
- Life insurance
- Pension benefits

WHAT IS AN OBITUARY?

An obituary is a notice of someone's death. It usually includes a short biography. Obituary notices are appropriate for a legal notification of death.

The funeral director works closely with the newspaper staff and can assist the family in seeing that the death is properly reported.

A charge is often made by newspapers when a death notice is placed in the obituary column.

OBITUARY INFORMATION

The funeral home will normally write the article and submit it to the newspaper. They may ask for the following information about the deceased:

- Age
- Place of birth
- Cause of death
- Occupation
- College degrees
- Memberships held
- Military service
- Outstanding work
- List of survivors in immediate family
- Give time and place of services
- Charities for memorial contributions

DOES THE DECEASED HAVE
TO BE EMBALMED?

Embalming is rarely required by law. However, many funeral providers require embalming if there is going to be a viewing or visitation or extended delay in burial.

Eliminating this service can save you hundreds, and sometimes, thousands of dollars.

WHAT SHOULD I KNOW ABOUT EMBALMING?

According to the U.S. Centers for Disease Control, embalming provides no public health benefit.

Embalming does not preserve the human body forever; it merely delays the rate of decomposition, depending on the strength of the chemicals and methods used, and the humidity and temperature of the final resting place.

Embalming is a physically invasive process in which special devices are implanted, and chemicals and techniques are used to give an appearance of restful repose.

Embalming is very popular in the United States and Canada. Embalming is considered a desecration of the body by Orthodox Jewish and Muslim religions. Hindus and Buddhists, or anyone else choosing cremation have no need for embalming.

Many funeral providers believe that seeing the body, after death, is a necessary part of the grieving process, even if the death was long anticipated.

WHAT KIND OF CASKET IS BEST?

Again, it is a personal choice. Caskets vary greatly in style and price. They may be constructed of metal, wood, fiberboard, fiberglass or plastic.

Caskets can vary in price from $2000 to over $10,000. Often, a casket is the single most expensive item you will buy if planning a "traditional," full service funeral.

WHAT IS A GASKETED OR SEALER CASKET?

Metal caskets are frequently described as "gasketed," "protective" or "sealer" caskets. These terms mean that the casket has a rubber gasket or some other feature that is designed to delay the penetration of water into the casket and prevent rust.

Wooden caskets are generally not gasketed and don't have a warranty for longevity.

Be aware that manufacturers of wooden and metal caskets usually warrant for workmanship and materials, but not longevity.

WHAT IS THE DIFFERENCE BETWEEN A BURIAL VAULT AND A GRAVE LINER?

Both burial vaults and grave liners are placed in the ground and the casket is lowered into it for burial.

The purpose is to prevent the ground from caving in as the casket deteriorates over time.

Typically, a grave liner is made of reinforced concrete and will satisfy most cemetery requirements. In fact, many cemeteries include a grave liner when you purchase a burial space. Grave liners cover only the top and sides of a casket.

A burial vault is more substantial and expensive than a grave liner. It surrounds the casket in concrete or another material and may be sold with a warranty of protective strength.

Most burial vaults are sold by a funeral provider and most grave liners are sold by a cemetery.

State laws do not require a vault or liner.

WHAT SHOULD I ASK ABOUT THE CEMETERY SITE?

Most cities have a municipal cemetery as well as several cemeteries owned by religious or private organizations.

- Consider the location of the cemetery and whether it meets the requirements of your family's religion.
- Check to see if the cemetery has any burial restrictions on burial vaults purchased some place else.
- Check to see if there are any restrictions on the type of monuments or memorials it allows.
- Find out if flowers or other remembrances can be placed on the grave.
- Ask about the cost of a burial site.
- Is there a cost to open the grave for interment and additional charges to fill it in?
- Is perpetual care included in the purchase price?

WHAT IS A VETERANS CEMETERY?

It is a National Cemetery. All veterans are entitled to a free burial in a National Cemetery, with a grave marker. Spouses and dependent children are also entitled to a lot and marker when buried in a National Cemetery.

There are no charges for opening and closing the grave, for a vault or liner, or for setting the marker. The family generally is responsible for other expenses, including transportation to the cemetery. For more information, go to www.cem.va.gov.

WHAT IS A MAUSOLEUM?

A mausoleum is a building or structure for casketed human remains, used in lieu of burial. Individual spaces are called crypts.

WHAT IS CREMATION?

Cremation is the process of reducing the body to ashes and bone fragments through the use of intense heat, anywhere from 1400 degrees to 1800 degrees Fahrenheit. The body is placed in a container, and then placed into a cremation chamber or retort. They are exposed to direct heat and flame. The process usually takes two to four hours.

Depending on the size of the body, the cremated remains weigh about three to nine pounds. The cremated remains are called cremains.

Cremation regulations vary from state to state.

IS A CASKET REQUIRED FOR CREMATION?

No. However, most crematories require that the body be placed enclosed in some sort of rigid, leak proof, combustible container.

There is a choice of affordable containers, including options from a simple pine or cloth covered casket to a hardwood casket.

CAN FAMILY WITNESS THE CREMATION?

It depends on the crematory. Many funeral homes and cemeteries do not have their own crematory, so they contract out the cremation.

Some crematories have a viewing room where the family can watch the body be loaded into the cremation chamber.

IS CREMATION A SUBSTITUTION
FOR A FUNERAL?

No, cremation is simply a method of preparing human remains for final disposition.

Some families opt to have a traditional funeral service before cremation and some families prefer to have a service after cremation. It's completely a matter of family preference.

WHAT CAN BE DONE WITH THE CREMATED REMAINS?

You have numerous options. You could:

- Inter remains in a cemetery plot.
- Give remains to a family member (usually in an urn or box).
- Scatter over private property.

WHAT IS A COLUMBIUM?

Many cemeteries have columbiums. They are designed to hold urns containing cremated remains.

A columbarium, often located within a mausoleum or chapel, sometimes freestanding, either indoors or outdoors, is constructed of numerous small compartments. Another option is burial of the urn. You might choose either a bronze memorial or monument.

There are some cemeteries that offer scattering gardens.

HOW MUCH DOES A CREMATION COST?

Generally speaking, cremation costs less than traditional burial services, especially if direct cremation is chosen, in which the body is cremated as soon as legally possible without any sort of services.

However, there is wide variation in the cost of cremation services, having mainly to do with the amount of service desired by the deceased or the family.

If an undertaker is used to transport the body, obtain permits, and file a death certificate, the fee for services could run over $1000. If a visitation or a funeral service is held before cremation, the charges will be higher.

A cremation can take place after a full traditional funeral service, which adds cost. The type of container used also influences cost.

DOES CREMATION REQUIRE A FUNERAL SERVICE?

Once again, this is a personal choice. Even though visitation and a funeral service with a body present may be held before cremation, many have found it more helpful to have a memorial service without the body present.

If you choose to have the body present for visitation or funeral service before the cremation, many funeral providers will rent a casket to you for the service and then transfer the body to an inexpensive cremation container after.

WHY IS HAVING A PLACE TO VISIT
SO IMPORTANT?

Having a place to visit the deceased provides a focal point for memorializing them. One of the basic human desires is to remember and to be remembered.

WHAT IF I WANT TO DONATE MY BODY TO A MEDICAL SCHOOL AS AN ANATOMICAL GIFT?

Medical schools and other accepting facilities have specific requirements for receiving an anatomical gift. It is a good idea to check with the facility (far in advance) prior to the need. Ask about their procedures and requirements.

Most of these facilities do want the body embalmed. They may also require that the body be in a certain physical condition. There may also be a charge for transportation to the facility.

GRIEF RECOVERY

It is healthy to recognize death and discuss it honestly with friends and relatives. When a person dies, there is grief that needs to be shared.

Expressions of sympathy and the offering of yourself to help others following the funeral are welcomed.

It is important that we share our grief with one another. Your local funeral director can help family and friends locate available resources and grief recovery programs in your area.

A FUNERAL CHECKLIST

When planning a funeral, try not to do everything yourself. Call on a family member or friend to help you make the following arrangements.

Notify:

- Doctor
- Coroner
- Funeral home
- Clergy
- Relatives and friends
- Pallbearers
- Insurance agents
- Banks
- Unions and Fraternal Organizations
- Organists

Select:

- Cemetery property
- Funeral service
- Casket
- Vault or outer container
- Clothing
- Flowers
- Music

A FUNERAL CHECKLIST, CONT.

- Thank you announcements
- Transportation
- Time and place for funeral
- Time and place for visitation

Provide:

- Vital statistics about the deceased
- Birth date
- Birthplace
- Father's name
- Mother's name
- Social Security Number
- Veteran's Discharge or Claim Number
- Education
- Marital status

A FUNERAL CHECKLIST, CONT.

In addition you will want to:

- Find addresses of all people who must be notified.
- Make arrangements for out-of-town visitors.
- Find someone to help answer sympathetic phone calls, cards and letters, as well as greet friends and relatives when they call.
- Decide appropriate memorial to which gifts may be made (church, hospice, etc.).
- Prepare list of distant persons to be notified by letter/or printed notice and decide which to send.
- Locate the will and notify lawyer and executor.
- Check carefully all life and casualty insurance and death benefits including social security, credit union, fraternal and military.
- Check promptly on all debts and installment payments, including credit cards. Some carry insurance clauses that cancel balances upon death.
- Notify utilities and landlord and tell post office where to send mail (if deceased was living alone).

GLOSSARY

Advance Directive — An instruction such as a Durable Power of Attorney for Health Care, a directive pursuant to patient self-determination initiatives, a Living Will, or an oral directive which states either a person's choices for medical treatment or, in the event the person is unable to make treatment choices, designates who will make those decisions.

Assisted Suicide — Assisted suicide refers to the situation in which a person requests the help of others, in the form of access to information or means, the means, and/or actual assistance, in order to end their own lives.

Burial Vault — A burial vault is a burial container, and sometimes called a grave liner. The vault or liner is placed in the ground before burial, and the casket is lowered into it at burial.

Conservator — A conservator is a person or corporation appointed by probate court to manage another person's property and financial affairs.

CPR — Cardiopulmonary resuscitation is an emergency method of life-saving. Artificial respirations and chest compressions are used to restart the heart and lungs.

Cremation — Cremation is the process of reducing the body to ashes and bone fragments through the use of intense heat.

GLOSSARY

DPAHC — Durable Power of Attorney for Health Care.

Durable Power of Attorney for Health Care — A legal document that allows an individual to appoint an agent to make all decisions regarding health care, including choices regarding health care providers, medical treatment, and, in the later stages of the disease, end-of-life decisions.

Ethical Will — An ethical will is distinct from its legal counterpart in that it is focused on conveying the writer's values and principals to the next generation.

Euthanasia — Euthanasia generally refers to situations whereby someone intentionally takes a person's life with a stated intent to alleviate or prevent perceived suffering.

Executor — The executor is a person appointed by a testator to carry out the terms of the will. If this person is a female she is referred to as an executrix.

Funeral — A funeral is a ceremony marking a person's death.

Gerontology — Gerontology is the study of the elderly, and of the aging process itself. It is to be distinguished from geriatrics, which is the study of the diseases of the elderly. Gerontology covers the social, psychological and biological aspects of aging.

GLOSSARY

Grave Liner — A grave liner is made of reinforced concrete and will satisfy most cemetery requirements. Grave liners cover only the top and sides of a casket.

Guardianship — Guardianship is a legal method used to insure that a person who is unable to make decisions on their own has someone specifically assigned to make decisions on their behalf.

Holographic Will — It is a do-it-yourself, handwritten will.

Hospice — It is a program of supportive care services providing physical, psychosocial, and spiritual care for dying persons, their families, and other loved ones.

Irrevocable Trust — It is a trust in which none of its provisions can be changed, nor can the trust itself be canceled by the grantor.

Joint Will — A joint will is made in conjunction with another's will and requires distribution of property in a certain way regardless of who dies first.

Living Trust — A living trust, also known as, inter vivos, is a trust that allows a person to put his assets into a trust which is managed according to instructions given by the person creating the trust.

GLOSSARY

Living Will — A Living Will is one type of advance directive. It outlines your wishes concerning end-of-life medical care. A Living Will pertains to artificial life support and is not implemented until a physician decides that the individual is terminal.

Mausoleum — A mausoleum is a building or structure for casketed human remains, used in lieu of burial. Individual spaces are called crypts.

Medical Proxy — A medical proxy is someone named to make medical decisions for someone else. A proxy is chosen for a person by agreement of the family, or close friend. A proxy should be someone who has a close relationship with the patient and who knows that person's medical wishes.

Mortuary — A mortuary is a privately-owned facility for the purpose of receiving and preparing dead bodies for burial or cremation.

Obituary — An obituary is a published public notice of someone's death.

Palliative Care — Palliative Care is the care given to people with chronic, often life-threatening illnesses, or after it becomes obvious that no cure is possible. Care focuses on symptom management, such as relieving pain or stopping nausea, enhancing quality of life and psychosocial needs.

GLOSSARY

Pour Over Will — A short will often used with a living trust stating that any property left out of the living trust will become part of (or "pour over", into) the living trust upon death.

Power of Attorney — A power of attorney is a document which gives another person the power to handle some or all of your financial affairs. An ordinary power of attorney ends when you become mentally incapable because of sickness or injury to handle your affairs.

Probate — A legal process that the courts use to transfer title to property and make sure your debts are paid after you die, whether you die with a will or without one.

Reciprocal Will — In a reciprocal will, each spouse's will is a mirror image of the other.

Residuary Estate — The residuary estate is the portion of a decedent's estate that is left after the payment of specific legacies, debts, and estate administration expenses.

Revocable Trust — A trust in which any of its provisions can be changed, or the trust itself can be canceled at any time by the grantor. The grantor receives income from the assets. A grantor is the person who transfers assets into a trust for the benefit of another.

GLOSSARY

Statutory Will — It is a simple will written according to state law.

Terminally Ill — This usually refers to people who are close to death with no possible recovery. It can also be defined as an incurable or irreversible condition that without life sustaining procedures, results in death within a relatively short time or a comatose state from which there can be no recovery, to a reasonable degree of medical certainty.

Testamentary Trust — A will can have a trust written into it, called a Testamentary Trust, which is set into motion by the Court after the will reaches a certain point of execution, and is used only after the death of the person whose estate it represents.

Trust — A trust is an agreement that arranges for another person, bank or trust company to manage or control your property for your beneficiaries. When you sign a trust agreement, you are handing over "legal title" or ownership of savings, stocks and investments or other property to this person or institution.

Will — A will is a legal document that outlines your wishes for the disposition of your estate after your death.

RESOURCES

American Bar Association
321 North Clark Street
Chicago, IL 60610
312-988-5000
www.abanet.org

Aging with Dignity
888-594-7437
www.agingwithdignity.org

National Hospice and Palliative Care Organization
1700 Diagonal Road, Suite 625
Alexandria, VA 22314
703-837-1500
www.nhpco.org

National Academy of ElderLaw Attorneys
1604 N. Country Club Road
Tucson, AZ 85716
520-881-4005
www.naela.com

National Funeral Directors Association
13625 Bishop's Drive
Brookfield, WI 53005
800-228-6332
www.nfda.org

INDEX

INDEX

Check out these other great titles in the Senior's Guide Series!

**The Senior's Guide
to Digital Photography**

**The Senior's Guide
to Dating (Again)**

**The Senior's Guide
to the Internet**

**The Senior's Guide
to eBay®**

**The Senior's Guide
to Easy Computing**

**The Senior's Guide
to Computer Tips & Tricks**